# STEAMERS of the FORTH

## Volume 1: Ferry Crossings and River Sailings

*by*
Ian Brodie

...rry *William Muir* was almost 58 years old and quite worn out. She had steamed 800,000 ... broken up at Charlestown. Taken on 22 June 1935, this picture shows her entering

CLACKMANNANSHIRE
STENLAKE LIBRARIES 7 Up

First published in the United Kingdom, 2004,
by Stenlake Publishing Ltd.
Telephone: 01290 551122
Printed by Cordfall Ltd. Glasgow, G21 2QA

ISBN 1 84033 307 3

A South Queensferry call was introduced on the Stirling steamer service from 4 June 1886, when, following negotiations with the town council, the Galloway Saloon Steam Packet Co. opened a long pier extending from the west arm of the town harbour. It is seen in the distance of this view, taken from the Forth Bridge. Following the addition of South Queensferry, the Stirling steamers were speeded up by omitting the calls at Bo'ness and Charlestown, a move that allowed *Edinburgh Castle* to include some firth work in her roster from 1901. This pier also handled volumes of day trippers out to view work on the Forth Bridge.

# INTRODUCTION

Together with a companion volume subtitled Firth Services and Excursions, this book tells the story of local passenger sailings on the River and Firth of Forth. The ferry crossings controlled by Parliamentary Acts are covered here, as are the river sailings and crossings commencing at Queensferry or operating upriver from there. Ferries governed by Acts of Parliament operated between North and South Queensferry (the Queensferry passage) and Burntisland (initially Pettycur) and Granton (formerly Newhaven). This second route was initially known as the Fife and Midlothian ferry. Other less important ferry crossings were in the hands of local landlords who appointed tenants to operate them.

Europe's pioneer steamboat, *Comet*, sailed on the Forth, and upriver services from Newhaven were quickly established as vital links in Scotland's transport system, providing a route to Glasgow and the West Highlands via the Forth & Clyde Canal. Steam was applied to all the ferries in the 1820s, either using dedicated steamers or with tugs towing the sailing vessels. Despite this, the lack of proper harbours was a major problem.

With the development of the railway network the Burntisland ferry became an integral component of the main line north, with railway terminology applied. Sailings to Granton were 'up' and those to Burntisland 'down'. The problem of goods trans-shipment was solved in 1850 by the introduction of the first train ferry in the world, and the Granton–Burntisland crossing became increasingly busy until the opening of the Forth Bridge in 1890. At Queensferry, the last express stagecoaches to Dunfermline used the crossing, while at Kincardine and Alloa early ferries had been in use to ferry cattle to the great Falkirk trysts. Although Stirling and Edinburgh were linked by rail in 1849, the importance of the river was such that seasonal tourist services to Stirling continued until 1907. The construction of the Alloa Swing Bridge in the 1880s produced cross-current problems for the steamers, the solution being for them to lower their funnels and masts and rush under the bridge at full speed ahead, rather than waiting for it to open. Steam tugs were commonplace in the nineteenth century, being used to tow sailing ships and fishing vessels in and out of port. Upriver at Bo'ness and Grangemouth these also doubled as cruise vessels in their spare time.

Ferry traffic was minimal after the opening of the Forth Bridge, but the crossings had to be maintained as parliamentary approval was required for their abandonment. The Queensferry passage was leased from 1890 to 1920, with the North British Railway paying a subsidy to the operator. Traffic increased again with the growth of road transport from the early 1900s. The motor bus operator to Queensferry even introduced an electric boat as an extension of the bus service in 1914, and this developed into the ferry service to Inchcolm, still a feature of the summer scene at Queensferry.

The railway was loath to invest in ferry improvements which increased road traffic at the expense of rail, but when a shipbuilder offered to build new ferries the solution was to lease the ferry to him and let him invest in the new ships. Thus the Queensferry passage was operated by a Dumbarton shipbuilder from 1934 until the opening of the Forth Road Bridge in 1964, when the Road Bridge Act included the necessary legislation to abandon the ferry passage. The Burntisland ferry was abandoned at the start of the Second World War, and future attempts to reinstate it have been short-lived. At Alloa and Kincardine the Kincardine Bridge of 1936 effectively killed off the ferry crossings.

The last two decades have seen a minor resurgence in excursions on the Forth, with the success of the Inchcolm ferry and its increasing use for other cruising. There have also been occasional visits from the preserved excursion ships *Waverley* and *Balmoral*.

Following the introduction of the train ferry between Granton and Burntisland in 1850, increasing volumes of goods traffic meant that additional vessels were required. *Balbirnie*, built by S. & H. Morton at Leith for £15,150, joined the fleet in 1861. At 199 feet long, and with staggered funnels and an extra set of rails, her extra carrying capacity made her a very useful vessel. *Kinloch* followed five years later from Glasgow builders A. & J. Inglis. *Midlothian* was built at Leith by Ramage & Ferguson, measuring 262 feet and weighing 920 gross tons. She entered service in 1881. This poor but rare picture shows, from left to right, *Midlothian*, *Kinloch* and *Balbirnie* at Burntisland.

The River Forth is highly tidal and at low water its constrictions caused problems for early steamer traffic. Passing Queensferry, the flood develops whirls towards the shores, and for the first hour, while the tide is flowing in midstream, it is still ebbing along the shores. Above Grangemouth there is a reverse flow known as the 'lek'. The flood tide almost reaches high water mark in four hours and then changes direction, leaking out for the next hour or so. This is followed by the second flood. The lek and the second flood are gentle compared to the first. The ebb is very fast and can rip through the windings at nine knots, reducing to three by the time it reaches Queensferry. It is slower along the shores. Lasting just over four hours, the ebb is followed by the lek running in, raising the water level two feet at spring tides at Kincardine. This is followed by a second gentle ebb. River steamers capitalised on this tidal pattern, the steamer in 1814 leaving Stirling assisted by the last of the lek, then for the greater part of the voyage through the windings steaming into the second flood. Before Alloa the ebb caught her and assisted her to about Bo'ness, after which she paddled through slack water to her destination. Although later vessels were much faster and more powerful, the practice of tackling the windings against a slight current continued. In early years the 'Fords of Stirling' (where the river could be forded at low tide) constituted a hazard until they were removed in the 1840s, and larger ships had little room for navigational error. Any deviation and they grounded in soft mud, although with a jab astern on the engines, and the assistance of the reverse current, they soon floated off. Such occurrences were common. The Queensferry passage ferries also had to cope with the tidal rip, and earlier ships had a choice of three calling-places on the south bank, making for whichever they could reach and then crawling up the shore to the one most suitable for the return journey.

As a teenager, Henry Bell of Helensburgh, the owner of *Comet*, Europe's first commercial steamboat, had worked as a joiner with the Bo'ness shipbuilders Shaw & Hart. When *Comet* needed her first overhaul he brought her there via the Forth & Clyde Canal. She gave the Forth's first steamer excursion (from Bo'ness to Leith), with a one-way ticket costing 7s. 6d. The *Edinburgh Courant* of 21 May 1813 commented: 'The *Comet*, a vessel worked by steam, and the first of the kind ever seen in this quarter, is at present lying in Leith harbour'. The potential for a river service was immediately realised, and by June 1814 Bell had placed the *Stirling Castle* in service between Newhaven and Stirling. By 1815 a second vessel, *Lady of the Lake*, was in operation, competing with the new Alloa-owned *Morning Star*. Competition remained intense until 1825 when Bell's firm merged with its Alloa rival to become the Alloa, Stirling & Kincardine Steamboat Co. (later the Stirling & Alloa Steamboat Co.), at which point Bell and his Glasgow partners sold out to local investors for £4,500. This picture shows the replica of *Comet* which was built in 1962, at Helensburgh Pier.

The Edinburgh, Glasgow & Leith Shipping Co. operated sailing smacks via the Forth & Clyde Canal to Glasgow, and also had an interest in the canal passenger boats. It had *The Tug* built at Port Glasgow in 1817 and steamed round the north of Scotland to the Forth. She towed the company's smacks as required, but also provided a passenger service from Newhaven to Grangemouth connecting with the canal sailings. Traffic grew and a second vessel, the second-hand *Dumbarton Castle*, joined the fleet in September 1819. The terminus was extended across the Firth, at first to Dysart, later Inverkeithing, and later again to Largo, providing the first Forth steam ferry crossings. The opening of the Union Canal to Edinburgh in 1822 inevitably affected the Grangemouth traffic and sailings became seasonal. By 1828 a vessel named *Lion* had taken over the service, maintaining it until October 1833 when she offered a short-lived ferry from Newhaven to Charlestown, connecting with Lord Elgin's rope-drawn railway to Dunfermline. This advertisement is for *The Tug*'s intercity service.

The 'broad ferry' crossing (oficially known as the Fife and Midlothian ferry) from the Stone Pier at Newhaven operated to a number of destinations, but principally Pettycur, which was the terminus of the Great North turnpike road. There were no low-water landings on the north shore and at low tide passengers were landed on the rocks by small boats, meaning that no coaches could be handled. An Act of Parliament of 1813 invested exclusive rights of ferry with the trustees, prohibiting any other vessels from operating between Newhaven (later Granton) and Pettycur/Burntisland. From 1819 there was competition from the Edinburgh, Glasgow & Leith Shipping Co. which ran to Dysart and Inverkeithing, ports either side of the trustees' exclusion zone, and in August the following year the trustees placed the second-hand Clyde vessel *Sir William Wallace* in service to Pettycur and Burntisland. Two new boats, *Edinburgh Castle* and *Thane of Fife*, were built at Port Glasgow for the service in 1821. By this time Kirkcaldy and Dysart had been added as ferry ports and the service operated distinct west and east passages. *Sir William Wallace* was wrecked at Burntisland in a gale in January 1825 and replaced the following year by the Leith-built *Earl of Kellie*, which operated until 1839, being replaced the following year by the Dundee-built *Queen*. The ferry was the subject of constant political infighting and never succeeded in improving its services. It was replaced by a privately introduced Granton to Burntisland ferry in 1844, whose Act of Incorporation included approval to abandon the Fife and Midlothian ferry, an advertisement for which is reproduced here alongside a view of Pettycur harbour.

### THE STEAM-BOATS,

Belonging to the Trustees upon the Ferries of NEWHAVEN, PETTYCUR, KIRKCALDY, DYSART, and BURNT-ISLAND,

Will commence to ply at the following altered hours, upon Friday the 12th of April current :—

WEST PASSAGE,

Including Newhaven, Pettycur, Burntisland, and Aberdour.

| | |
|---|---|
| From Burntisland for Newhaven, at | 6 A. M. |
| Newhaven for Pettycur, with Fife coach passengers, | 7 — |
| Pettycur to Newhaven, by Burntisland and Aberdour, | 8 — |
| Burntisland to Aberdour, | 8¾ — |
| Aberdour to Newhaven, at | 9 — |
| Newhaven to Burntisland, with Perth coach passengers, | 10½ — |
| Burntisland to Newhaven, with ditto, | 11½ — |
| Newhaven for Pettycur, at | 1 P. M. |
| Pettycur for Newhaven, with Fife coach passengers, at | 3 — |
| Newhaven to Aberdour and Burntisland, | 4 — |
| Burntisland for Newhaven, at | 5 — |
| Newhaven for Pettycur and Burntisland, | 6½ — |

EAST PASSAGE,

Including Newhaven, Pettycur, Kirkcaldy, and Dysart.

| | |
|---|---|
| From Newhaven to Kirkcaldy and Dysart, at | 6 A. M. |
| Dysart, back to Kirkcaldy, at | 8 — |
| Kirkcaldy to Newhaven, at | 8½ — |
| Newhaven for Pettycur, Kirkcaldy, and Dysart, at | 11 — |
| Kirkcaldy to Newhaven, calling at Pettycur, at | 3½ P. M. |
| Pettycur for Newhaven, at | 4 — |
| Newhaven to Kirkcaldy and Dysart, at | 5 — |
| Dysart to Kirkcaldy, at | 6½ — |
| Kirkcaldy to Newhaven, at a quarter before | 7 — |

It is recommended that passengers will be at the ferry stations before the hours of sailing, as fixed by this table, the superintendents having instructions to keep strictly to the fixed hours, weather permitting.

SUNDAYS.

A Steam-boat will sail from Newhaven to Pettycur, touching at Burntisland, at 9 and half past one P. M.; and from Pettycur to Newhaven, touching at Burntisland, at half past 10 A. M. and three P. M.

This 1811 map shows piers and landing places associated with the Queensferry passage. In 1809 an Act was passed for the improvement of this passage, giving exclusive rights of ferry to the trustees and providing a government loan of £10,000. Four large sailing boats were introduced, capable of carrying coaches and horses, and new piers were built at the Battery and Longcraig on the north shore, while on the south shore Newhalls (later known as the Hawes) was improved and new landings made at Port Edgar and Longcraig. The ferry lost two thirds of its coach traffic after the introduction in 1820 of steamships on the Pettycur crossing, and as a result ordered a steamboat from Menzies of Leith. Named *Queen Margaret*, she entered service on 1 October 1821, towing the sailing boats in addition to carrying her own traffic. In 1836 she was replaced by the iron paddle steam tug *William Adam* from the same builders. Subsequently the crossing suffered from the lack of railway connections, and in September 1864 the trustees leased the passage to John Croall, the proprietor of the largest surviving fleet of stagecoaches. He placed the tug *Benwell* on the crossing, but she was burnt out while lying at North Queensferry, and *Nymph*, a former Mersey ferry, replaced her, carrying Scotland's last express stagecoach which operated until Croall's death in 1873. Upriver, the Kincardine and Alloa ferries carried large numbers of cattle destined for the Falkirk trysts. The Alloa steam ferry was introduced by the Earl of Mar and Kellie in 1823 using a double-ended catamaran vessel 75 feet long. Cattle rates were fixed at 4*d.* per beast, dropping to 3*d.* if there were seven or more. At Kincardine Lord Keith carried out pier improvements and introduced the steamboat *Tulliallan Castle* in 1829. This was at Alloa by the 1830s when two new boats were built for Kincardine. However, the opening of the railway from Stirling to Perth in 1848, and the introduction of a cattle market in the latter town, reduced traffic on these ferries, and the steam service at Kincardine was withdrawn at the end of 1852 with the ferry continuing using sailing boats only. At Alloa, the steamboats were declared unseaworthy the same year, and a small steamer called *Jane* introduced by J. Falshaw of Perth. She was withdrawn three years later when the ferry reverted to operation by sailing craft. From 1865 the Caledonian Railway held the tenancy of the Alloa ferry, and in 1869 the Earl of Mar and Kellie persuaded the railway to reintroduce a steamboat. The result was *Countess of Kellie*, a small double-bowed paddle steamer which operated until made redundant on the opening of the Alloa Swing Bridge. She was sold in 1885 to David MacBrayne for coal carrying, and replaced by a small steam launch, *Lord Erskine*, owned by Alex McLeod, the local tug master, running until her replacement by a larger vessel in 1905.

# BURNTISLAND & GRANTON FERRY.

## WINTER HOURS.

 On and after TUES-DAY, 1st OCTOBER, and until further no-tice, the New STEAM-  BOATS on the GRANTON and BURNTIS-LAND FERRY will depart from each side as follows :—

| FROM GRANTON. | FROM BURNTISLAND. |
|---|---|
| 1st Boat at 50 min. past 5 A M. | 1st Boat at 15 min. past 7 A.M. |
| 2d do. at 30 " " 8 A.M. | 2d do. at 9 A.M. |
| 3d do. at 30 " " 10 A.M. | 3d do. at 30 " " 10 A.M. |
| 4th do. at 12 noon. | 4th do. at 12 noon . |
| 5th do. at 2 P.M. | 5th do. at 25 " " 3 P.M. |
| 6th do. at 5 M.P. | 6th do. at 30 " " 5 P.M. |

## SUNDAY HOURS.

| FROM GRANTON. | FROM BURNTISLAND. |
|---|---|
| 1st Boat at 50 min. past 5 A.M. | 1st Boat at 8 A.M. |
| 2d do. at 30 " " 9 A.M. | 2d do. at 1 P.M. |
| 3d do. at 15 " " 2 P.M. | 3d do. at 25 min. past 3 P.M. |

*N.B.*—In order to secure regular Embarkation, it is necessary that Carriages, Carts, Horses, Cattle, and Goods should be on the Piers not less than Fifteen Minutes before the departure of the Boats.

For the Proprietors,
**PETER WORK,** Superintendent at Burntisland.
**JAMES HUME,** Superintendent at Granton.

Sir John Gladstone of Fasque, Kincardineshire, father of William Ewart Gladstone, wanted to improve the Fife ferry, and in the late 1830s leased a plot of land east of Burntisland harbour with this in mind. He entered into a partnership with the Duke of Buccleuch, who had recently opened Granton harbour, and on 30 June 1842 a Parliamentary Act was obtained to build a pier at Burntisland and provide three steamships for a ferry to Granton, with a minimum of eight daily crossings in summer and six in winter. Two ferries were ordered from J. B. Maxton of Leith, one for £4,800, the other with second-hand engines for £300 less. These were named *Burntisland* and *Granton*. A Clyde steamer called *Maid of Leven* was purchased as a third vessel for £1,250. The investment totalled £38,000 and the service commenced on 5 September 1844, carrying 922 passengers that first day. By 5 July 1845 it had conveyed 35,999 passengers; 828 carriages; one sedan chair; twenty-five corpses and hearses; 4,259 carts, wagons and vans; 4,608 horses; 40,972 farm animals of all types; and 9,077 loose barrels, bottles, caskets, chests, puncheons, hogsheads and parcels. The ferries proved slow, taking up to forty-five minutes for the crossing, and a fourth ship was ordered from a Cheshire yard for delivery in 1847. On building its line across Fife from Burntisland, the Edinburgh & Northern Railway (E&NR) purchased the crossing for £90,000 (over twice what it had cost) and took over the working on 1 January 1847. This advertisement for the ferry details its winter hours.

The fourth ferry ordered by Gladstone was named *Forth* and was delivered to the crossing's new owners, the Edinburgh & Northern Railway, in April 1847. She proved just as slow as the other vessels, but the railway was so desperate for additional carrying capacity that it accepted her. Radical action was required, however, and two new passenger ships were ordered from Thames builders. Named *Auld Reekie* and *Thane of Fife*, they were in service by March 1848. A second-hand vessel, *Comet*, dating from 1838, was also purchased from the same builders, while another boat, costing £15,500 and named *Express*, joined the fleet as its flagship in spring 1849. Originally flush-decked, aft saloons with promenade facilities above were added to the four new vessels between 1851 and 1858. These were, of course, exclusively for the use of first class passengers! *Forth* was retained as a spare, *Comet* sold and the other original vessels classified as goods boats. The passenger service was thus established for the next 25 years. In 1849 the E&NR was renamed the Edinburgh, Perth & Dundee Railway, and absorbed into the North British Railway (NBR) in 1862. This picture shows either *Thane of Fife* or *Auld Reekie* at Burntisland, with the train ferry *Carrier* at the jetty on the right.

The problem of how to trans-ship goods and minerals between trains and steamers was given much consideration. Initially the railway ordered a dumb barge (a vessel with no engines which would be towed across the river), but this was never used, and the revised plan was for a flat-decked steamer with railway tracks fitted on deck, the wagons being lifted on and off by crane. Such a vessel was ordered from Robert Napier of Glasgow in March 1848. Just prior to her launch, however, the company appointed the young Thomas Bouch (of first Tay Bridge notoriety) as manager, and he quickly convinced a sceptical railway board that wagons could be loaded using a chain-operated flying bridge (a drawbridge fitted with rails), with the

wagons being winched on and off. Called *Leviathan*, the first train ferry in the world was introduced using this technology and commenced operations on 1 March 1850 between Burntisland and Granton. A similar but smaller vessel, named *Robert Napier* after her builder, was delivered in November for service across the Tay, but in fact spent much of her life on the Burntisland crossing. The original goods ferries were soon disposed of, and Bouch reported that in its first thirteen months the train ferry carried more than 29,000 wagons. This pioneering technology prompted an article in the *Illustrated London News* of 9 February 1850, from which this engraving is reproduced. (*By courtesy of the Trustees of the National Library of Scotland.*)

In 1868 the Board of Trade had reduced the number of passengers the ferries at Burntisland were permitted to carry, and thereafter the route was operating at capacity and extra tonnage was required. Spare vessels from the Clyde (*Dandie Dinmont*) and the Solway (*Carham*) were tried unsuccessfully, and eventually a new ferry was ordered from Key's of Kinghorn. Named *John Stirling* after the NBR chairman, she was a handsome vessel, and at 190 feet was 40 feet longer than any of the previous ferries. She is seen here at Burntisland in 1876, her first year of service, along with *Nymph* (see page 7). *Nymph* was purchased from John Croall's executors by the NBR in 1873 and continued on the Queensferry passage until 1877, when she was reboilered and used as a tug at Charlestown. She was probably undergoing repairs, as Burntisland was the repair and servicing centre for the railway ferries.

*John Stirling* was found to be rather a wet ship, and in November 1876 was fitted with bilge keels and a large forecastle, providing useful covered accommodation for livestock and horses. She is seen here leaving Burntisland.

*Express* (see page 9) was sent to Key's for reboilering in January 1878, and once slipped was found to be in terrible condition. A new ferry was therefore built round her replacement boilers and *Express* scrapped. Called *William Muir*, and seen here at Burntisland, the new vessel was a smaller and neater edition of *John Stirling*. She was launched in October 1879 with steam up, after which *Forth* was immediately sold and broken up.

In 1867 the train ferry ramp at Burntisland, originally situated beside the passenger pier, had been moved to the east end of the harbour, nearer the goods marshalling yard, as seen here. With the collapse of the first Tay Bridge in December 1879, plans for a bridge over the Forth were cancelled and improvements to the train ferry became imperative. At Burntisland a long sea wall was built to provide more shelter.

*Midlothian* was built at Leith by Ramage & Ferguson, and at 262 feet long and 920 gross tons was much the largest ferry of her day. She cost £27,600 and was in service by the autumn of 1881. Her capacity of 40 wagons represented an increase of about 40 per cent on previous vessels, and allowed the small ferry *Carrier* to be sold for service to the Isle of Wight. This picture shows *Midlothian* at Burntisland.

Although plans for a bridge over the Forth were initially dropped after the Tay Bridge disaster, confidence in the project subsequently re-emerged. The Forth Bridge opened on 4 March 1890, and following this the NBR withdrew its train ferry service between Granton and Burntisland, while at the same time passenger sailings on both the Burntisland crossing and Queensferry passage were reduced to the legal minimum. At South Queensferry the harbour and station at Port Edgar were closed, as were the railway pier and station at North Queensferry. On 24 April the Queensferry lease and *John Beaumont* (see front cover) were sold to Captain Arthur for £1,250. *William Muir* was retained by the railway to operate the Granton–Burntisland ferry and all other vessels were disposed of. *Auld Reekie* and *Thane of Fife* went to Norway, where the former was immediately scrapped, the latter sinking in Bergen fairway on 14 September 1893. Having been sold to an Edinburgh agent, *John Stirling* operated on the new Manchester Ship Canal in 1894, while the train ferries *Leviathan*, *Balbirnie* and *Kinloch* were all broken up. *Midlothian* lingered for almost a decade before being towed to Sweden and scrapped there. Construction of a wet dock at Burntisland between 1897 and 1900 involved the destruction of the ferry piers, and in 1898 a new pier was built on to one of the old coal wharfs. The passenger slip at Granton remains to this day, but the main high water pier became the base for the lighthouse tender and was rebuilt in 1909. No trace remains of the train ferry berths. This photograph shows *John Stirling* and *Carrier* at Burntisland 1876.

Leith wine merchant John Kidd entered the firth excursion trade in 1874, and in 1876 appointed ship chandler Matthew Galloway, also from Leith, as his manager. Concurrent with this he took delivery of two new steamers, designed specifically for the Stirling trade. These were *Lord Elgin* and *Lord Mar*, built at Stockton-on-Tees. They were fine steamers measuring 160 feet long, with raised quarterdeck design giving a spacious saloon aft. A promenade forward provided covered accommodation for steerage passengers. Despite their attractive design they were slow, their advanced compound diagonal machinery being insufficiently powerful. On 22 April 1876 *Lord Elgin* and *Lord Mar* commenced a daily service to Stirling, calling at Limekilns, Bo'ness, Kincardine, Alloa and (from 1878) Dunmore. With three single trips daily, river residents were also able to make a return journey to Leith. There was insufficient traffic for two ships, however, and in 1878 *Lord Elgin* was deployed down firth; then on 29 March 1879 *Lord Mar* left the Forth and sailed to Pernambuco (now Recife) in Brazil. That summer the Stirling service was reduced to four days per fortnight, with departures from Leith between 10 and 11.30 a.m. John Kidd died on 29 April 1880 and the following spring his executors sold *Lord Elgin* to Bournemouth owners. She later passed to the Southampton, Isle of Wight & South of England Royal Mail Steam Packet Co. (today's Red Funnel), and in 1921 was converted into a cargo carrier running five days per week from Southampton to Cowes. She was withdrawn in 1953 and broken up two years later. At the time of her withdrawal she was the oldest paddle steamer in Britain, with 77 years of service. No photographs are known to exist of her on the Forth, and this picture shows her at Swanage in Dorset.

The tugs *Transit* and *Blue Bonnet* maintained the Stirling service in 1881, and for the following season Matthew Brydie of Alloa purchased the Loch Lomond steamer *Princess of Wales*, seen here at Luss. She was a pretty ship, with an elegant saloon on the after-deck, and her deck extending three feet over the hull to provide passageways around the saloon. Construction of the swing bridge above Alloa had commenced that April, however, and the work was partly blocking the river and causing strong cross eddies. *Princess of Wales* was too large to pass safely and was laid up from 19 August, the Leith tug *Fiery Cross* taking over the service, being small enough to squeeze past the bridge works. On 1 August 1883 *Princess of Wales* reappeared, being chartered by Walter Beveridge of Alloa, but conditions were little better and she collided with the bridge that day, causing considerable damage to both structures.

It seems probable that *Princess of Wales*'s saloon was so badly damaged that it was removed, and she reappeared in 1884 as a flush-decked steamer with an awning over the aft deck. By that summer conditions at the bridge had improved and the Stirling sailings resumed. However, after Walter Beveridge died suddenly on 2 May 1885 his sons transferred *Princess of Wales* to Dundee, where renamed *Albion* and later *Shamrock* she became a well-loved vessel for the next quarter of a century. This photograph of her at Newburgh shows her after transfer to the Tay.

A partnership was formed by John Kidd's executors named the Forth River Steam Shipping Company, again with Matthew Galloway as manager, and after Robert Croall of the coaching family joined the business in the winter of 1883/4 the decision was made to resume the river service between Leith and Stirling. Built by S. & H. Morton at Leith, *Stirling Castle* was 160 feet long with 'furnishings tastefully designed to attract the better class tourist . . . the upper saloon [is] cushioned in olive green velvet, the dining saloon in crimson velvet and the forecabin in haircloth'. She sailed on a proving run on 29 March 1884, but on slowing to half speed was caught by a side current and smashed into the Alloa bridge works. Having been repaired she entered service on 1 May, sailing only as far as Alloa, from where connecting coach tours were offered. Typically passengers could sail to Alloa and take a coach to Dollar, rejoining the steamer at Kincardine. Inclusive fares were from 4s. to 4s. 6d. By 1886 *Stirling Castle* was sailing to Stirling.

The bridge contractors took S. & H. Morton to court seeking damages for careless navigation, but their case was dismissed, the contractors being severely censured for interfering with the river navigation in contravention of the Alloa Railway Act. The bridge had upset the flow of the tide, causing strong cross eddies, and it proved impractical for passenger steamers to stop and wait for it to open. The only way to avoid being caught by the cross currents was to pass under it at full speed, so in 1885 *Stirling Castle* appeared with a fold-down mast and telescopic funnels. The company's *Lord Aberdour* was also so-fitted as a spare vessel, and a new steamer, *Edinburgh Castle*, was similarly equipped.

On 9 April 1886 the Forth River Steam Shipping Co. was dissolved and reregistered as the Galloway Saloon Steam Packet Co., with Thomas Aitken of the London & Edinburgh Shipping Co. as chairman, and Matthew Pearson Galloway as managing owner. The steamer livery was changed from the prosaic black hull and black-topped yellow funnel to mauve hulls, white paddle boxes and navy yellow funnels. (At this period naval vessels on service in the tropics had white hulls and deep yellow funnels. The colour specified for those on the Galloway Co.'s vessels was thus 'navy yellow'.) From 1887 the 1886-built *Edinburgh Castle* became the regular Stirling steamer, remaining so until 1907 – apart from during 1890 when the service was maintained by the smaller *Lord Aberdour*, a move which led to a large number of complaints. Built by J. Scott of Kinghorn, *Edinburgh Castle* was a modern ship with – for the first time on a Forth steamer – her deck saloons extended to the full width of her hull. This greatly increased both saloon accommodation and promenade deck space. The Stirling terminus was at the shore, from where *Edinburgh Castle* is seen ready to leave. She gave a return run daily, Monday to Saturday, the times changing to suit the tide and with sailings sometimes commencing from Stirling rather than Leith.

The Stirling service was suspended after the 1907 season (the only year when *Stirling Castle*, dating from 1899, provided it) when the NBR, which had owned the company since 1889, adopted a policy of containing the steamer services to areas which did not compete with the railway. The run through the windings was one of the high points of the trip from Stirling, followed by the section of the route round the Alloa inches (islands), passing under the Alloa Swing Bridge with the funnel telescoped and the mast lowered. Alloa was the first call, and the firth cruise steamers gave excursions from there on public holidays. Steamers then continued to Kincardine, Bo'ness and Charlestown, the latter added to the river calls from 13 August 1889 after the NBR granted the lease on the old steamboat berth on the outside wall of the harbour. Upriver Sunday cruises were introduced by *Stirling Castle* in 1902 via Queensferry, Bo'ness and Kincardine, some continuing into the windings. These were continued by *Redgauntlet* from 1909–14. Following an early sail from Leith, she occasionally offered day cruises from Alloa via all the piers to Methil and the Bass Rock. This picture shows *Edinburgh Castle* in the windings.

*Edinburgh Castle* leaving the Galloway Co.'s pier at South Queensferry. The year is 1889 or 1890, with the Forth Bridge almost complete.

Traffic on all the ferries was minimal following the opening of the Forth Bridge in 1890, although as the twentieth century progressed an increase in road traffic led to something of a renaissance. During the lull following the opening of the railway bridge, tourists and day trippers became an increasingly seasonal portion of the ferries' revenue at both Burntisland and Queensferry. In 1893 the ferry at Queensferry was leased to John Wilson of Bo'ness and gave frequent cruises, while at Burntisland the railway-owned *William Muir*, still painted in the black livery of the pre-bridge days, was smartened up in 1902 when repainted in the NBR's Clyde livery of red funnels with black stay ring, white band and black top, but with white paddleboxes. She is seen here leaing Burntisland.

Thus smartened up, *William Muir*, seen here at Granton, began to attract day trippers. This funnel livery is worn today by the preserved paddle steamer *Waverley*.

B 1865  Ferry S.S. William Muir leaving Burntisland.

By 1910 the 31-year-old *William Muir* was worn out, and that year she retired to Ramage & Ferguson's Leith yard for a major refit, emerging unrecognisable. Her fore funnel and boiler had gone, leaving extra open space for road vehicles. She had new paddles and boxes, new compound diagonal engines fed by twin boilers astern of the engines, and was now good for another quarter century of work. This picture shows her at Burntisland.

John Wilson of Bo'ness acquired the Queensferry lease after Captain Arthur retired in October 1893, the NBR providing an annual operating subsidy of £375 (reduced in 1910 to £300), plus an interest-free loan of £1,250 to finance a suitable ferry. Wilson purchased the 32-year-old former Tay ferry *Forfarshire* (seen here at Hawes Pier) and she maintained the service for over twenty years, giving frequent cruises round Inchgarvie Island to view the bridge between ferry crossings. In 1904 she was reboiled, receiving the absurdly tall funnel shown in the photograph.

FERRY PIER, NORTH QUEENSFERRY

In 1908 the service was augmented by the purchase of *Woolwich* from the Great Eastern Railway. Built in 1890, she was 100 feet long, and her arrival allowed the crossing to handle vehicles all year round, duties being shared with *Forfarshire*. This photograph of *Woolwich* was taken at North Queensferry town pier.

ALLOA FERRY, W.T. & CO. 40

During the early years of the twentieth century ferry traffic from the sawmills at South Alloa was increasing, and in 1905 the 63-foot twin-screw *Hope* (illustrated here) replaced the small launch on the Alloa ferry. Latterly she was fitted with ramps to carry one lorry, but ceased running on the opening of the Kincardine Bridge in 1936. The sailing boat ferry between Kincardine and Higginsneuk also ceased at this time, but the Alloa crossing was taken over and continued by James Bremner using the 35-seater launch *Sunbeam*, purchased from Largs on the Clyde. The service finally ceased on his call-up for war service in December 1939.

There were a number of small towage companies around the Forth, often serving dedicated ports. At Grangemouth the firm of J. & G. Mackay & G. Pederson was formed into the Grangemouth & Forth Towing Co. by its executors in 1886. From about this time the company offered a meagre programme of about a dozen excursions each season using its tug *Jupiter*, sailing from Grangemouth old dock, usually with a connecting train from Falkirk Grahamston. Sailings were provided daily during the Falkirk trades holiday in early July. The former Clyde tug *Flying Owl*, renamed *Forth*, took over this work in 1902 when *Jupiter*'s certificate was allowed to expire. Thereafter there was a long midsummer gap in the excursions, as from about 10 July until late August *Forth* was stationed at Berwick-on-Tweed (where this photograph was taken) to tow the fishing fleet in and out of harbour. Between times coastal excursions were given from Berwick. These were suspended during the First World War, but *Forth* reappeared as a passenger ship on 1 July 1919 with a cruise to Leith and Aberdour. Frequent cruises from Grangemouth followed, including one to the Galloway Co.'s pier at South Queensferry, the last call to be made there. In 1920 *Forth* was joined by another former Clyde tug, *Runner*, and over thirty day, afternoon and evening cruises were given from Grangemouth, the frequency reducing to about twenty the following year. Destinations included Kirkcaldy, with a passing call at Aberdour. *Forth* was withdrawn at the close of the 1923 season and broken up at Alloa. There were a few cruises from Grangemouth subsequently, particularly during the Falkirk trades holiday, given from 1927 by the excursion steamer *Fair Maid*. These were abandoned after the 1933 season.

John Wilson, who operated the Queensferry passage from 1893, also had the NBR towing contract for the railway's harbours at Bo'ness, Charlestown, Burntisland, Methil and Tayport. He owned a gaggle of elderly tugs and most of them had passenger certificates. *Royal Norman* (illustrated here) was the best known at Bo'ness for excursion work and gave afternoon or evening cruises each Wednesday and Saturday. There was also a Wednesday evening cruise from Hawes Pier, Queensferry, given by *Admiral* or *Perogomez*. If numbers were within her firth certificate she sailed downstream, but if busier the trip was upstream to Brucehaven or Bo'ness. If there were altogether too many passengers for the tug, it took over the ferry while the ferry provided the excursion.

*Flying Fish* at Bo'ness. During the annual holiday week in mid-July, three of John Wilson's vessels gave daily excursions from Bo'ness to destinations ranging from Elie Point or May Island to Stirling, while a fourth offered trips from South Queensferry. *Flying Fish*, a former Clyde tug, was popular on the longer cruises. Wilson arranged cruises for all manner of events including the Stirling and Alloa games, fairs at Kincardine or Culross (Blair Pier), and Kirkcaldy band contest. From 1905 the new dockyard at Rosyth provided a focal point for many a cruise, while from its opening in 1909 the Marine Gardens at Portobello proved a big attraction, reached by steamer to Leith and thence by tramcar.

John Wilson also operated many charters on behalf of groups including the Old Boys' Athletic FC, the Rechabites, the Good Templars and the YMCA. Most of these cruises were open to the public. This picture shows *Admiral* ready to sail from Bo'ness with the 1898 outing of the Bo'ness and Carriden United Free Church Choir.

In 1906 John Wilson acquired the redundant Clyde river bus *Clutha No. 6*, his only purely passenger vessel, and that summer she sailed daily from Grangemouth giving cruises to the windings, Culross, or the training ship *Caledonia* off Queensferry. Thereafter she was mainly used on charters, and this photograph shows her at anchor off Inchcolm. Wilson's cruises came to an abrupt end in mid-July 1913 when Board of Trade regulations requiring increased life-saving equipment on all passenger-carrying vessels came into force, following the loss of the White Star liner *Titanic*. Wilson was not prepared to spend the money, and signed dispositions at the customs' office that he would in future only use his vessels for towing duties. The Galloway Co.'s *Redgauntlet* sailed from Bo'ness throughout the 1914 holiday week, and the company also gave sailings from Grangemouth on the Falkirk May and July holiday Mondays that year.

The Burntisland to Granton ferry was suspended from 1 January 1917 on Admiralty orders, and *William Muir* was later requisitioned for minesweeping duties, serving at Sheerness from June 1917 until May 1919. The ferry service resumed on 16 July 1919 after a hurried refit. John Wilson had died on 3 February that year, and his executors sold out to the Leith Salvage & Towage Co. which decided that it wanted to dispose of the ferry obligations. The NBR resumed direct working of the Queensferry passage on 13 November 1920, having purchased the former Tay ferry *Dundee*. Though 45 years old she had been reboiled in 1914 and was in excellent condition. She was certificated to carry 997 passengers, three lorries and two motor cars, with a maximum unit load of five tons. When loaded she drew 4 ft 6 in, and at spring tides was unable to operate for two and a half hours either side of low water. The town pier at North Queensferry was also unsuitable due to lack of water, and the service moved to the railway pier, to which the Admiralty had conveniently built a road. Fares were increased, a move which required statutory approval, and to make this increase permanent the railway (by this time the LNER, having absorbed the NBR in 1923) undertook to improve the service by 50 per cent. Pier works costing £21,835 were carried out, with a 250-foot extension added to the Hawes and the end of the railway pier at North Queensferry lowered. This reduced the maximum service gap to two hours, but in practice the ferry usually operated, even if berthed across the end of Hawes Pier and unable to load vehicles. Extra summer working hours were also introduced. This picture shows *Dundee* at the Hawes Pier.

E 364   The Forth Bridge

The Scottish Motor Traction Co. (SMT) had been running motor coaches from Edinburgh to Queensferry since 1906, and in 1914 introduced *Electric Arc* on bridge cruises. She had been built at Dumbarton in 1911 to the order of Mr Mavor of the electrical engineering firm Mavor & Coulson, and is reputed to have been the first electrically driven vessel in the world. During the war she was employed as a Rosyth liberty and mail boat, and while on this service went on fire, her blazing hulk being beached near Port Edgar. Replacements *Auld Reekie* and *Cramond Brig* were introduced in 1921 and restarted the cruises from Hawes Pier, where the latter was photographed. While one provided short 'view the bridge' trips, the other sailed on ninety-minute cruises to view Rosyth dockyard and Blackness Castle. The latter route was replaced in 1925 by an Inchcolm service, the Ministry of Works having agreed to open a tea room on the island, which the company advertised as 'the Iona of the East'.

The short bridge cruises ceased after 1934 when *Cramond Brig* was sold to Millport owners, but *Auld Reekie* continued on the Inchcolm service until the completion of an anti-submarine boom from Cramond Island to Inchcolm put an end to her sailings on 24 August 1939. On at least one occasion she also deputised for the Burntisland ferry, and is seen here entering Burntisland. She operated as a tender to the boom and was sold to the Ministry of War Transport on 17 August 1942, later being renamed *Symphony*.

Sir Maurice Denny, anxious to keep his Dumbarton shipyard busy, approached the LNER in 1933 with a proposal for new ferry boats for Queensferry. The railway response was that if he built the boats on his own account, they would give him the lease of the ferry. He did, and from 1 March 1934 William Denny Bros. operated the Queensferry passage. Two outwardly identical new vessels were introduced: *Queen Margaret* (illustrated here leaving Hawes Pier) and *Robert the Bruce*. They were double-ended, side-loading to suit the existing slipways, with capacity for 28 cars and a high bridge amidships with sufficient clearance for a furniture van. Diesel electric machinery drove each paddle wheel independently through a chain drive, giving a speed of nine knots. They could cope with the tide, but always displayed three black discs on their signal lanyard as a sign to other shipping meaning 'Out of control, keep clear'.

While *Queen Margaret* was of conventional riveted construction, her sister *Robert the Bruce* was the first Clyde-built ship to be entirely electrically welded, thereby allowing comparisons to be made of the economy and performance of a welded hull. Under Denny's operation, vehicle rates were reduced, the cost for a car coming down from 10s. to 4s. A 30-minute service was provided, the vessels passing each other in mid-river. Between 1934 and 1948 (the period of two-ship operation) 99.3 per cent of the crossings were made on time. This photograph shows *Robert the Bruce* leaving Hawes Pier.

Queensferry passage letterhead showing *Robert the Bruce*.

# QUEENSFERRY PASSAGE

TELEPHONE:
SOUTH QUEENSFERRY 253.

TELEGRAMS:
PASSAGE, SOUTH QUEENSFERRY.

FLEET
"QUEEN MARGARET."
"ROBERT THE BRUCE."
"MARY QUEEN OF SCOTS."
"SIR WILLIAM WALLACE."

Manager:-
R. A. MASON, .M.Inst.T.,
HAWES PIER,
SOUTH QUEENSFERR
WEST LOTHIAN.

*Dundee* was loaned to Denny as a spare vessel, and with her funnel painted black appeared early each year while the new ferries were overhauled. The rest of the year she was laid up in Burntisland harbour. Latterly, like many old ladies, she became rather eccentric, and on a few occasions was carried up- and downstream by the current. This picture shows her leaving Hawes Pier during her final weeks of service in April 1948.

The ferry that replaced *William Muir* was the Wallasey Corporation vessel *Snowdrop*, dating from 1910. While being towed round the north of Scotland from the Mersey, she broke loose off Cape Wrath and was adrift for over two days. Alterations for the Burntisland crossing included a general stiffening to obtain the appropriate certificate, and cutting back her forward promenade deck to give space for cars. Renamed *Thane of Fife* she entered service on 3 March 1937. The Burntisland ferry was suspended during the Second World War from 20 March 1940, but *Thane of Fife* remained on the Forth on tender duties at Granton (where she is seen entering the harbour) and Port Edgar. She was laid up in 1946, first at Bo'ness and later at Alloa while parliamentary authority was obtained to abandon the crossing. After this had been granted she was sold to a Glasgow buyer and was broken up at Passage West, Cork in 1949. There are rumours that she was involved in carrying emigrants to Israel, but no proof of this has been found.

Volumes of road traffic continued to grow following the Second World War, and in November 1947, with *Dundee* ailing, Denny agreed to provide a further ferry for the Queensferry passage, although shortages were such that she was not in service until the spring of 1950. Called *Mary Queen of Scots* (seen here approaching Hawes Pier), she was identical in appearance to Denny's earlier pair of vessels, but didn't have the electric drive, her diesel engines being connected by chains to the paddles. On her arrival *Dundee* was handed back to the railway (by then British Railways) and scrapped. A twenty minute service was provided, with a ship at each pier and one crossing.

The press announced plans to reopen the Granton–Burntisland ferry on 13 March 1949, and for the next two seasons the Inchcolm excursion launch *Forth Lady* ran a morning and evening service from Granton to Burntisland on Wednesdays, Saturdays and Sundays. John Hall, a Kirkcaldy baker, was originally behind the scheme, but he sold his interest before the service started to a new concern called Forth Ferries Ltd. Share capital was £29,701, and Sir Andrew Murray, Lord Provost of Edinburgh, was chairman. Four surplus tank-landing craft were purchased and converted by James Lamont & Co. of Port Glasgow. They were well laid-out with a tea lounge, cocktail bar and sheltered boat deck, while the open car deck could accommodate thirty to forty cars. The first ship, *Bonnie Prince Charlie*, arrived in Granton, where this photograph was taken, on 18 July 1950, but there were long delays thereafter in starting the service.

By the end of 1950 Forth Ferries had taken delivery of *Flora Macdonald* and *Glenfinnan,* together with the passenger vessel *Ulster Lady* which returned from service on the Clyde. *Eriskay* completed the fleet early in 1951. The service finally got going on the April holiday weekend, and after a shaky start was operating a thirty minute service by summer, with *Ulster Lady* acting as passenger overflow vessel at the weekends, crossing with a pile of bicycles on her saloon roof. Here, *Glenfinnan* is leaving Granton.

Winter traffic was disappointing, and the long delays in starting the service had stretched the finances of the company. By the end of 1951 it had liabilities of £272,901, and on 14 October 1952 the Court of Session, at the instigation of Granton Harbour Ltd., issued a warrant arresting *Flora Macdonald* for unpaid harbour dues. The service frequency was reduced to hourly, being suspended entirely after the 8 p.m. run on 12 December 1952. *Flora Macdonald* acted as tender to the liner *Batory* in July/August 1953, but otherwise the fleet remained laid up. The ferries were sold for service as ore carriers at Marmagoa, Goa, with two leaving Granton under tow on 28 February 1954 and the final pair following on 3 August. *Ulster Lady* remained laid up in the Old Dock at Leith until sold for scrap in October 1955. The ferry briefly restarted during a rail strike in June 1955, with the small Burntisland-based motor launches *Victory* and *Skylark* providing a service. It did not outlast the rail strike. Taken in September 1951, this photograph shows *Ulster Lady*, *Bonnie Prince Charlie* and *Flora Macdonald* at Granton.

A fourth ferry, *Sir William Wallace*, was added to Denny's fleet in 1956, after which both sides of Hawes Pier were used by the ferries. The building of the Forth Road Bridge brought an influx of visitors to South Queensferry, and in the summer of 1960 Denny Bros. brought their shipyard tug/tender *The Second Snark* to Queensferry and restarted bridge cruises. Still sailing on the Clyde, she is a comfortable vessel with two small saloons and accommodation for 128 passengers upstream (calm water) or 105 downstream (moderately calm water). From 1961 her cruises were extended to include a short call at Inchcolm, and two years later a morning cruise was added from Granton as part of an Edinburgh city coach tour. This picture shows *Robert The Bruce*, *The Second Snark* and *Sir William Wallace* at Hawes Pier in 1962.

## QUEENSFERRY PASSAGE

NOTICE.—Your attention is specifically drawn to the Conditions of Carriage as posted on the Ferry Vessels, Office and contained in this folder.

# TOLLS & CHARGES
## PAYABLE IN RESPECT
## OF FERRY TRAFFIC

**1. Motor cars (for private use)**

| Engine c.c.'s 1947 and later | Horse Power pre 1947 | | |
|---|---|---|---|
| 1 to 1,000 | 1 to 8 | . . . . | 4/6 |
| 1,001 „ 1,700 | over 8 „ 13 | . . | 5/3 |
| 1,701 „ 2,500 | „ 13 „ 18 | . | 6/3 |
| 2,501 „ 3,000 | „ 18 „ 29 | . | 7/3 |
| 3,001 and over | „ 29 | . . | 8/3 |

(Above charges include the driver, charged at 7d.)
Season Tickets are issued in the same relation of engine c.c.'s to pre 1947 horse power ratings as shown above:—

| Engine c.c.'s | One Month | Three Months | Six Months | Twelve Months |
|---|---|---|---|---|
| 1 to 1,000 | £4 14 | £12 13 | £22 13 | £34 2 |
| 1,001 „ 1,700 | £5 14 | £15 4 | £27 4 | £40 14 |
| 1,701 „ 2,500 | £7 2 | £19 3 | £34 2 | £50 17 |
| 2,501 „ 3,000 | £8 9 | £23 0 | £40 17 | £61 0 |
| 3,001 and over | £9 18 | £26 16 | £47 11 | £71 3 |

(Charges quoted above include the driver. Passengers charged additional as shown in Section 17 hereof.)

**2. Mechanically-propelled goods, vehicles, including tractors, agricultural vans and lorries and dual purpose vehicles.**

| | Unladen | Laden |
|---|---|---|
| Not Exceeding 1 ton (Unladen Weight) | 5/9 | 8/- |
| Exceeding 1 ton but not exceeding 1½ tons | 6/9 | 11/- |
| „ 1½ tons „ „ „ 2 „ | 8/6 | 14/- |
| „ 2 „ „ „ „ 2½ „ | 10/- | 17/- |
| „ 2½ „ „ „ „ 3 „ | 12/- | 21/6 |
| „ 3 „ „ „ „ 4 „ | 16/- | 30/6 |
| „ 4 „ „ „ „ 5 „ | 20/- | 40/- |
| „ 5 „ „ „ „ 6 „ | 23/6 | 50/- |
| „ 6 „ „ „ „ 7 „ | 28/- | 60/- |

(Above charges include driver)

**Notes**

(a) Maximum unladen weight of goods vehicles accepted for transport, 7 tons.

(b) No vehicle having a total weight exceeding 11 tons is accepted for transport.

(c) A vehicle shall be classed as "laden" and charged for as such if it conveys any load of merchandise of whatever weight not being part of the normal equipment of the vehicle.

## TOLLS & CHARGES—Contd.

(d) In the case of vehicles carrying empties only, used, or to be used in connection with traffic conveyed by the ferry, the above rates of charges shall be reduced by half of the difference between the unladen and laden charges.

(e) Heavy vehicles can only be accommodated if the space is available in a safe place on the vessel.

(f) Charges on goods vehicles are based on the unladen weight shown on the Road Fund License.

**3. Motor vehicles paying hackney Carriage license duty**

| Seated for | | |
|---|---|---|
| Not more than 4 persons | . . . | 5/9 |
| More than 4 persons but not more than 8 | . | 7/6 |
| „ „ 8 „ „ „ „ 14 | . | 9/3 |
| „ „ 14 „ „ „ „ 20 | . | 12/- |
| „ „ 20 „ „ „ „ 26 | . | 14/- |
| „ „ 26 „ „ „ „ 32 | . | 15/6 |
| „ „ 32 „ „ „ „ 40 | . | 16/9 |
| „ „ 40 „ „ „ „ 48 | . | 18/- |
| „ „ 48 „ „ „ „ 56 | . | 20/- |
| „ „ 56 „ „ „ „ 64 | . | 22/- |
| „ „ 64 pro rata, but not more in any case than | . | 30/- |

(Above charges include driver, and conductor if any, each charged at 7d.)

**4. Motor Bicycles**
Under 100 c.c.'s 1/9 (including driver)
Over 100 c.c.'s 2/3 (including driver)
Season tickets will be issued at the following rates:—

| | Under 100 c.c.'s | Over 100 c.c.'s |
|---|---|---|
| One Month | £ 1 18 6 | £ 2 15 0 |
| Three Months | £ 4 13 6 | £ 6 12 0 |
| Six Months | £ 8 5 0 | £12 2 0 |
| Twelve Months | £14 0 0 | £20 0 0 |

**5. Motor cycle with side car, motor cycle car or motor tricycle 4/–** (including driver, passengers additional as in Section 17 hereof.)

**6. Pedal bicycle or tricycle 1/2** (including rider)
Season tickets will be issued at the following rates:—

| Pedal cycle and rider | — One Month | £ 1 10 9 |
|---|---|---|
| „ „ „ | — Three Months | £ 4 5 3 |
| „ „ „ | — Six Months | £ 6 18 0 |
| „ „ „ | — Twelve Months | £11 0 0 |
| | Tandem, 2/3 (including riders) | |

**7. Trailers, of whatever nature, drawn by private motor cars 1/9d. per foot of length including tow bar.**

**8. Trailers, of whatever nature, drawn by commercial goods vehicles or tractors.**

| Unladen | . . | 1/–per foot of length ( including |
|---|---|---|
| Laden | . . | 1/6 „ „ „ „ ( tow bar |

**9. Hearse, motor or horse-drawn**
10/– (driver included in both cases, charged at 7d.)

**10. Corpse, 12/6**

**11. Motor or horse drawn ambulance**
6/6 (including driver, charged at 7d.)
Season ticket will be issued at following rate:—
Ambulance Twelve Months £50 0 0

## TOLLS & CHARGES—Contd.

**12. Animal-drawn vehicles (excluding agricultural implements) drawn by less than four horses.**

| Private | 2 wheel | . . . | 5/- |
|---|---|---|---|
| | 4 wheel | . . . | 7/- |
| Commercial | laden, 2 wheel | . | 6/6 |
| | laden, 4 wheel | . | 8/6 |
| | unladen, 2 wheel | . | 5/- |
| | unladen, 4 wheel | . | 7/- |

(Above charges cover draught animals, and include driver, charged at 7d.)

**13. Hand truck or barrow**
Empty, 1/9, Laden, 2/3 (includes attendant)

**14. Perambulator or mail cart (not folding)**
1/6 (including attendant)

**15. Invalid chair (hand or motor-propelled)**
2/3 (including owner)

**16. Wheeled agricultural implements**
1/6 per foot of length

**17. Passengers**
Except as indicated elsewhere in this Schedule, every passenger above 12 years of age 7d. Up to 12 years of age, 4d.
Season tickets will be issued at the following rates:—

| One Month | . . . | £0 17 0 |
|---|---|---|
| Three Months | . . | £2 6 3 |
| Six Months | . . | £4 0 0 |
| Twelve Months | . . | £6 1 0 |

**18. Animals**

| Horses (excluding stallions), mules and asses | 2/6 each |
|---|---|
| Stallion | 8/- „ |
| Cow, ox or heifer | 1/6 „ |
| Bull | 5/- „ |
| Calf, sow or hog | 1/3 „ |
| Sheep or goat | 6d. „ |
| Lamb or kid | 4d. „ |

**19. Special Sailings by arrangement with the Manager** on giving not less than two days' notice.

**20. Notes**

(a) Explosives or highly inflammable substances are not accepted for transport.

(b) All tickets available on journey of issue only.

(c) CONCESSIONARY FARES are available for private cars, vehicles for public hire (i.e. hackney carriages and buses) and to passengers using both QUEENSFERRY and TAY FERRY IN SUCCESSION. A rebate voucher is issued when paying tolls on first ferry and on presentation at second ferry within one week from date of issue, a 20 per cent rebate is allowed on both fares.

(d) Parcels will be carried at owner's risk charged at:— Up to 1 cwt., 1/- per parcel, plus 1/- for each 1 cwt. or fraction of 1 cwt. in excess.

Queensferry passage tariff from 1963.

The liquidation of Denny's shipbuilding business in 1963 didn't affect the ferry service, which continued until the opening of the Forth Road Bridge on 4 September 1964. Two days later *Queen Margaret* made a symbolic last run with 500 passengers on board, when this photograph was taken.

With services suspended, the ferries were returned to the Caledonian Steam Packet Co. (on behalf of British Railways) and laid up at Burntisland. Seen here, left to right, are: *Queen Margaret, Mary Queen of Scots, Robert the Bruce* and *Sir William Wallace*. The first two were broken up at Inverkeithing in March 1965, and the following month *Robert the Bruce* ended her days at Bo'ness. *Sir William Wallace* sailed via Southampton to become a cargo carrier on the Dutch Islemeer, and was broken up at Ghent in March 1970. In November 1963 *The Second Snark* had been purchased by Brown Bros. of Edinburgh for use in tank stabiliser research. However, for the summers of 1963 and 1964 she operated excursions from Granton in connection with Corporation Coach Tours, followed initially by a run to Queensferry, but traffic there was disappointing and operations were confined to Granton by midsummer. She thereafter returned to her research duties, based at Cockenzie harbour, returning to the Clyde on 29 May 1969. She is still in service there as a tender and summer cruise vessel.

Big-time cruising returned for a few days in May 1981 when *Waverley* visited the Forth. She is seen here at Grangemouth, loading for a cruise via Granton round the Bass Rock. She visited again the following year but in 1983 her sailings were restricted to departures from Granton and Burntisland. She has not been back since, but in 1989 the motor-ship *Balmoral* paid her first visit to the Forth, which included a cruise to Bo'ness for a trip on the preserved steam railway, and a cruise from Grangemouth. She has returned most years since, but did not sail from river ports again until 2001 when she commenced firth cruises from Rosyth, following the closure of Burntisland harbour. Cruises off Grangemouth have been given when the weather has prevented more open-water work, the most recent being in 2002.

In 1981 John Watson purchased the Burntisland-based launch *Victory*, and having renamed her *Maid of the Forth* restarted the Inchcolm service from Hawes Pier. He replaced her the following year with the twin-screw *Maid of Bute*, which became *Maid of the Forth* (II) and is seen here approaching Hawes Pier. She had been built at Fraserburgh in 1937 for John Knox of Rothesay and had latterly been sailing from Fort William. Her passenger certificate was for 100 passengers, class six; 134, class five.

*Maid of the Forth* (III) was custom-built for Forth cruising at Bristol and made her maiden voyage to Inchcolm in May 1988. She is 19 m long, with 6 m beam and 1.5 m draught. Her passenger certificate is for 225 passengers. Built for the Inchcolm service, she can also pass under the closed Kincardine Bridge and has performed a number of charters upriver, some of which have commenced from Limekilns and Aberdour. The launch *Serenity* was also run in 1993 as a ferry providing transport to the then new Deep Sea World at North Queensferry. John Watson retired in 1993 and his vessels were purchased by Colin Aston, who has added evening jazz cruises to the programme from a variety of departure points. *Maid of the Forth* (III) is seen here on an evening jazz cruise calling at the pier at Blackness Castle in July 1997 to pick up a group from the South Queensferry Rotary Club.

The Granton–Burntisland ferry restarted in 1991 with the catamaran *Spirit of Fife* and dedicated bus connections to central Edinburgh. She came from the Channel Islands and was built in 1988 as *Herm Trident*. With capacity for 250 passengers, she was reported to have carried 90,000 in 1991 alone. By 1993 sailings were spasmodic, and she was laid up at Granton after tendering to *Queen Elizabeth 2* on 13 June 1993. The company then went into liquidation. This picture shows her approaching Burntisland.